STORM
SWIMMER

STORM SWIMMER

ERNEST HILBERT

WINNER 2022 VASSAR MILLER PRIZE IN POETRY

University of North Texas Press
Denton, Texas

Printed in the United States of America.

10 9 8 7 6 5 4 3 2 1

Permissions:
University of North Texas Press
1155 Union Circle #311336
Denton, TX 76203-5017

The paper used in this book meets the minimum requirements of the American National Standard for Permanence of Paper for Printed Library Materials, z39.48.1984. Binding materials have been chosen for durability.

Library of Congress Cataloging-in-Publication Data

Names: Hilbert, Ernest, 1970- author.
Title: Storm swimmer / Ernest Hilbert.
Other titles: Vassar Miller prize in poetry series ; no. 30.
Description: Denton, Texas : University of North Texas Press, [2023] |
    Series: Number 30 in the Vassar Miller prize in poetry series
Identifiers: LCCN 2022045936 (print) | LCCN 2022045937 (ebook) |
    ISBN 9781574418958 (paperback) | ISBN 9781574419023 (ebook)
Subjects: LCGFT: Poetry.
Classification: LCC PS3608.I4175 S76 2023 (print) | LCC PS3608.I4175
    (ebook) | DDC 811/.6--dc23/eng/20220926
LC record available at https://lccn.loc.gov/2022045936
LC ebook record available at https://lccn.loc.gov/2022045937

Storm Swimmer is Number 30 in the Vassar Miller Prize in Poetry Series

Cover image, "La Furie" by Chilean artist Franco Salas-Borquez, oil on canvas, 65×122 inches, 2021, from a private collection.

The electronic edition of this book was made possible by the support of the Vick Family Foundation.

For Ian

CONTENTS

Acknowledgments   xi
Storm Swimmer   1

1.

Pelagic   5
Last Star   6
In the Hidden Places   8
Bound Demons   9
December Issue   10
Vertebrate   11

2.

We Make Mountains So We May Move Them   15
Stronghold   16
Voltage Crackles at the Edge   17
Laurel Hill   19
Last Rites   20
K 265   21

3.

Air and Water   25
She Abides with Me Still   26
Riddle Me   27
Martini Shot   28
Demon   29
West River Notebook   31
Interlude—Weathering   32

4.

On Cape Charles   35
Visitations   37
Spolia Opima   38
From the Balcony on Heavy Metal Tribute Night
     at the Trocadero   40
Range   41
Drink Me   42

5.

Union Lake   45
Remains   47
Scream Queen   49
We Regret   50
Appeal   51
Monster-mania Con 44   52

6.

Endless Mountains   57
Lodge   58
Great Egret over Lake Luxembourg   60
EL CONQUISTADOR   61
The Inlet   63
In Paradisum   65

7.

Alchemericana   69
Salvaging   70
Mineral Springs Trail   71
Deep Shade   72
In Salt Meadows   74
Sole Unquiet Thing   75

ACKNOWLEDGMENTS

I extend warmest gratitude to the editors of the magazines in which these poems originally appeared, some in slightly different forms, including *32 Poems, Asheville Poetry Review, Bennington Review, Bowery Gothic, Cassandra Voices, The Dark Horse, Edinburgh Review, Fruita Pulp, Hawk & Whippoorwill, Hopkins Review, Hudson Review, Literary Matters* (Association of Literary Scholars, Critics, and Writers), *Measure Review, Modern Age, The Moth, The New Criterion, The North American Anglican, ONE ART: A Journal of Poetry, Per Contra, Philadelphia Stories, Raintown Review, Red Fez, Seneca Review* (50th-Anniversary "On Anxiety" Edition), *Smartish Pace, The Spectator, THINK: A Journal of Poetry, Fiction, and Essays*, and *Trinity House Review.*

I wish to thank all those who have assisted me with suggestions and criticisms of the poems in this book at various stages, and to make special acknowledgment of the following: Alicia Stallings (with special thanks for coining the title "Alchemericana" as a misreading in an email exchange), Sunil Iyengar, Amy Glynn, Luke Stromberg, John Wall Barger, Ashley Anna McHugh, David Yezzi, and Bill Coyle. Thanks also to Dora Malech and Eduardo Corral for their generous support of the book. Deepest gratitude to Rowan Ricardo Phillips for believing in this book and to John Poch for overseeing the competition in which it was selected as winner. Thanks to Franco Salas Borquez for his enthusiasm and the use of his painting *La Furie* (2021). Thanks also go to his gallerist, Mitch Plotkin of M Fine Arts Galerie (Boston / Palm Beach). Special thanks to William Smith of the US Department of Justice for safely and sagely tutoring me in the use of a Glock 19, 9mm as I worked on the poem "Range." Thanks to David Shoukry for sharing his knowledge of Renaissance Italian musical forms. "Riddle Me" was written specifically as NFT (nonfungible token) art, listed for sale on OpenSea, a peer-to-peer marketplace for rare digital items and crypto collectibles housed at the Hunter College MFA program in New York City. It was posted for sale on March 18, 2021, and sold to a private collector on July 2 the same year. The poem "Last Rites" appeared as a limited-edition letterpress broadside, issued by Tollund Press of Essex County, Massachusetts, in summer 2021 in an edition of twenty-four numbered copies, signed (four copies *hors de commerce*), with artwork provided by Ian, the author's son. The poem "Pelagic" appeared as a limited-edition letterpress broadside from Tollund Press in summer 2022 in an edition of sixty numbered copies with art provided by Franco Salas Borquez, six signed and sealed in bottles, three to be deposited into the gulf stream. "Appeal" was selected as a Laureates' Choice winner in the 2021 Maria W. Faust Sonnet Contest, Great River Shakespeare Festival.

"Lodge" is for Lynn. "K 265" is for David Yezzi. "Monster-Mania Con 44" is for my brother, David. "EL CONQUISTADOR" is for Quincy R. Lehr. The poems are all for my son, Ian, who inspires me in "restoring / With a new verse the ancient rhyme." "*In Paradisum*" is for Derick Dreher, who loaned us his space heater when our furnace failed. This book is also dedicated to fellow poets and other practitioners of *ars notoria*. The epigram from Giacomo Carissimi (1605–1674) can be translated as "my heart is a sea of tears," a line from the *duetto* "Partenza dalla sua Donna." The poem "Remains" does not refer to any real place or history. Lancelot Andrewes described "solsitio brumali" as "the very dead of winter" or the winter solstice. The Latin term "*spolia opima*" translates as "rich spoils" and refers to the trophies a Roman general stripped from the corpse of an enemy slain in single combat. "*Stercus Diaboli*" is "the Devil's shit." William H. Race translates the epigraph to this book, from the *Argonautica*, as:

> And likewise the other heroes boarded and took their seats
> in order and grasped the oars in their hands. Argus loosed
> for them the stern cables from under the sea-washed rock.
> Then they began striking the water mightily with their long
> oars. At evening, on Orpheus' instructions, they put in at
> the island of Electra, Atlas' daughter, so that by learning

secret rites through gentle initiations they might sail more safely over the chilling sea. Of these things, however, I shall speak no further, but bid farewell to the island itself and to the local divinities, to whom belong those mysteries of which I am forbidden to sing.

The epigraph to chapter seven is from book five of *The Odyssey*, translated by Samuel Butler as: "Thereon he floated about for two nights and two days in the water, with a heavy swell on the sea and death staring him in the face; but when the third day broke, the wind fell and there was a dead calm without so much as a breath of air stirring."

βαῖνον ἀριστῆες: λάζοντο δὲ χερσὶν ἐρετμὰ
ἐνσχερὼ ἑζόμενοι: πρυμνήσια δέ σφισιν Ἄργος
λῦσεν ὑπὲκ πέτρης ἁλιμυρέος. ἔνθ' ἄρα τοίγε
κόπτον ὕδωρ δολιχῇσιν ἐπικρατέως ἐλάτῃσιν.
ἑσπέριοι δ' Ὀρφῆος ἐφημοσύνῃσιν ἔκελσαν
νῆσον ἐς Ἠλέκτρης Ἀτλαντίδος, ὄφρα δαέντες
ἀρρήτους ἀγανῇσι τελεσφορίῃσι θέμιστας
σωότεροι κρυόεσσαν ὑπεὶρ ἅλα ναυτίλλοιντο.
τῶν μὲν ἔτ' οὐ προτέρω μυθήσομαι: ἀλλὰ καὶ αὐτὴ
νῆσος ὁμῶς κεχάροιτο καὶ οἳ λάχον ὄργια κεῖνα
δαίμονες ἐνναέται, τὰ μὲν οὐ θέμις ἄμμιν ἀείδειν.

—APOLLONIUS OF RHODES, *ARGONAUTICA*

It is not the distance from shore, but the depth, that marks
the transition to the true sea . . .

—RACHEL CARSON, *UNDER THE SEA-WIND*

Time, like the sea, unties all knots.

—IRIS MURDOCH, *THE SEA, THE SEA*

STORM SWIMMER

Without the sun the sea is tangled steel.
No colors survive where waves hike and freeze
The beach and batter the old boards behind.

Brash gulls—they raided all summer—have departed,
Discarding the scene to relentless roar
And hiss, unending crescendo. There is

No point to towels or other kinds of comfort.
Heels sting in marl that loosens like cubes of ice.
The churned-up pits of ocean sear the skin.

Sand slithers. The undertow sucks the shins.
Hail spikes the neck. It's hard to stand. The sky
And shore are gone. Clamp your eyes. Dive.

1.

PELAGIC

I face an ocean, its lurid rush and pull
The same as ever, though I have aged.
I step in—small cool splashes on my calves—
Then shoulder through hard linebacker waves.
I dive beneath a breaker and surface
In hissing warm swells, brine on my lips again.

I swim a while, then break to breathe and float
In foam. A clouded yellow butterfly
Has trailed me out and veers nearby. It spins
And banks above, my body its nearest ground.
It lights on my chest, wings unhurriedly
Closing like bellows. I strive to stay still.

It's off, fast as a blink, alive in the sun.
I spin over, face down in the lapping
Amber glass, the pelagic summer roll
Of original sea, the sandy glint
Of bubbles climbing in the goggle's pane,
My arm swiping down in time like a fluke,

Mottled in swarming undersea light.
The breakers roll in to hide the beach from me.
I imagine I'm in a world only
Ocean and sky, four billion years ago
Or in a time to come, floating without
The earth to save me, as long as I might.

LAST STAR

Another storm will be here soon.
Winds drive older snow to a dune
    Against the fence. The weeds
    Wait for spring. Darkness leads
The eye into a half-gone moon.

Winter creeper and bull thistle,
Though dead for the time being, bristle
    And spike. Bindweed and birch
    Still smother stems and search
For ground to cover on this hill.

Vines looped themselves around barbed wire
All summer. Now the strangling sweetbriar
    Sleeps in muddy banks of snow;
    Once winter's gone, they'll grow
Again like an untended fire.

To live for not yet created things
Is to live in an air that brings
    Dawn through winter trees,
    Sharp air that makes lungs freeze,
And sense a song though no bird sings.

Can one live in that deadly air
Before the light, without an heir
    Or benefactor,
    Without thought, fact or
Unreal whims, or much of a prayer,

And believe what's yet to be?
We survive by what we cannot see
    Because it isn't here
    Yet—hope that answers fear—
As ash in earth sustains a tree.

At the horizon, light will seep.
Most, in warm beds, are still asleep.
    Out here, in cold, the weed
      Aspires to come back, feed
On waste, reach farther, and grow deep.

IN THE HIDDEN PLACES
In solsitio brumali

Bach's *Mass in B Minor*
Haunts with its cathedral heights
The all-day dawn of snowstorm,

Ghosts of singers and song, composer
Of winter's depths whose flights
Of light gather to new forms.

Through the cold pane
We watch a while, and hear,
As the scene we know is changed

By a cold white whose reign
Is whole and pure as time, the year
At its nadir, our zone rearranged

And remote from the sun
Whose light hardly reaches this far
Side of the untended earth. The air

Will be dirty enough today to darken
Our portico, which halfway faces that faint star
As it slips its shadows by inches up the stair.

BOUND DEMONS

I notice my finger's bleeding only when I
Spot the smears and fingerprints along
The margins. There, outside the type-thick wood,
The snowy fields are marred with red, a sky

Aluminum above, a sense of dread as strong
As surf that pulls me through the book. I should
Just put it down. The end is in the teared-
Up trolley's window—rainy darkness, smudged

Streetlights. Electric crystals slide and flare.
I close the book and seal the blood, pages paired
And trapped together now. My stop. I'm nudged
With those who jostle with me down the stair

Into the storm, umbrellas snap, blown up and out,
The torrent drenching hair and socks. Inside
My bag the book embraces blood and drought,
Lightning and loss, and all I have to hide.

DECEMBER ISSUE

The margins of the magazine are home
    To curious archipelagos
Of butter dripped from poorly balanced toast.
    See, here's an ad that shows a book

That no one's going to buy, and no one read,
    A vanity, a squandered year.
The bars are closing down, the restaurants dead.
    Helicopters, humming, beam the lawn,

And shots are heard, and men are killed; each night,
    The tallies climb to make the news.
A patch of snow holds on amid the leaves.
    It slides toward the gurgling drain.

The radio brings lessons and carols
    From King's College, Cambridge,
"And the darkness comprehended it . . ."
    While bad news piles up behind.

The light is longer, Christmas not yet here,
    But feels as if it won't arrive,
Receding mists of hill and hill, cascades
    Of gray each day to dark.

A slosh of budget rye will torch the throat
    But hardly help dispel the dread.
The skies are cold and dull again today.
    We must remember all our dead,

The fragrant wreaths of years gone past entombed
    In trash, the cards torn up, first breath
Of air exhaled from flesh exhumed.
    A child has come to conquer death.

VERTEBRATE

I stretch on a tattered rug, turning my spine.
Sometimes I feel immense as fossil remains

Of a pilot whale washed ashore, dense layers
Of blubber and organs torn by gulls,

Devoured from below by tropical things
That slime their way up out of the drenched sand,

Until only the marble vertebrae
Remain under ribs that rock up like vaults,

Polished white by sun. Jellyfish are caught
As if in teeth, dried until invisible.

Terrestrial crabs with furry black legs
Scale and descend all day like workmen.

Warm surf splashes up and slithers back down
Through thoracic castles, where once much pain,

And longing, and an essential flicker
Of life's movement and radiance ran through—

Sheltered by shadowing leaves of coconut palms,
Aquatic song of rising sunset winds,

Bumped by newborn bulbs of beach hibiscus,
Crowded with busy fronds of sea lettuce—

No more the vast call of seething cold gulfs
Aswarm with sustenance, no zoom of fluke,

Smothered now by common purslane, sinking
Hiss of sand that slowly swallows the great spine.

2.

WE MAKE MOUNTAINS
SO WE MAY MOVE THEM

In Tolstoy's *Cossacks*, all around, snow
And a pebble sun brightening for miles.
It's one of my November books,
Filled at its start with white and cold.

Today sun lights up the house. Soon
We'll have snow too. Bob Dylan's
Highway 61 Revisited in the speakers
Jangles as it did a half a century ago.

My wife dangles our baby till he squeals,
Both nearly strangled with laughter,
And I take off my glasses to watch them.
He wants to fly and never be put down.

We will one day be stars above a storm,
As we were once diamonds in the ocean,
Tiny, tough parts of the world that flicker
And ascend and give up all our light.

STRONGHOLD

Christmas is picked clean, only balsam resin
Streaked on the jamb, a glint of tinsel.
For Christ's sake, it's hardly even seven
In the morning and sirens peal
In Doppler down the embankment below.

My blinds are drawn against the muddy dawn.
I don't want to look, don't even want to know
Who it is or what the hell's going on.
Whoever it is, he's at it pretty early.
I know he's probably been up all night

Or for a few days and nights. Surely
He's had a good time. He puts up a fight.
I wonder if he'll get away. I'd like
To stretch like a lion across the bed
All day, but I hear my young son's awake.

Our home is messy, warm, twice bolted.
My heir to these creaking halls of dusty air,
Black bells of heavy clouds looming above,
Carefully stepping down from stair to stair—
I haven't got a thing to give but love.

VOLTAGE CRACKLES AT THE EDGE

There's thunder in the sun. So says
My son. He says a lot of things
He knows must not be true

But wishes that they were,
And so do I—dragons ride in the dump truck,
The cat is wearing my coat, the sky

Is filled with cottage cheese,
The doggies row a boat, the baby bear
Is in the bath, that we'll live forever

And always be in love, right here, like this,
With waves that fly out
Ninety million miles to light

Up the book we read together.
My son's eyes are big. He says we have
To whisper or monsters might come in.

He's not afraid of ghosts. For him,
They're only things that can't be seen.
And what is to be feared in that?

He thinks that he's a ghost when hiding
Behind the window curtain, though
He cannot resist the giggling fits

That give him away and back to us again.
We're ghosts. We are. You're right,
My little one. We're ghosts,

But filled with spirit fire
That floats from somewhere else
And keeps us here for now

And when we're only ghosts
I know we'll stay in love, like now,
Because we lived by love,

And took from love our magic lives—
Objects bending time and space,
Alone with what we love.

LAUREL HILL

The boy sits down at the mausoleum
As if it's a porch, just like any other,
Despite classical vault and entablature,
Egyptian ornaments to suit a museum
Façade or hall of mummies. His mother
Catches up to him. She peeks in the embrasure

Above the gate. Late sunlight this autumn
Afternoon inches into advancing dark. The breeze
Is warm, one of the last of the season,
Awakening and confiscating leaves

From nursing branches. To the boy, it's
A big old-fashioned house where someone lives.
He taps politely on the stained glass.
Leaves blow and collect where he sits.
His mother's hand appears, and he gives
Her his. They walk off on long-shadowed grass.

LAST RITES

I've known beauty almost impossible
To believe, nearly always lost amid
All the usual distractions. Deadlines loom.
Taxes come due. Birthdays pass. Debts double.
But once a bright and late summer sun filled
The air, angling astonishingly through a room

Filled with music, some old heart-aching song,
And there was my son, not yet two years, coming
Across the floor toward me with arms outspread,
His face big with a smile, and he was so strong
And new, unworried blue eyes, becoming
Ever giddier, unbalanced, lunging ahead,

Hoping to fly in that warm light with his father,
To hug me as if for very life, and I wished I could
Stay there always lifting him, laughing, and such
Light linger as if we're still together,
And I will tell you it hurt it was so good,
And I know I've had that. I had that much.

K 265

Our house is filled with stars. Our son, just turned
Three, peels tiny blue decals from a sheet
Of constellations and decorates the piano,
Literary magazines, the kitchen floor.

He sings his song, a song that's many songs,
Just as he's composed of many moods and minds,
Many words for one melody: a song
We all know, the "Alphabet Song," and so

We're taught to read and speak, though it's also
"Twinkle, Twinkle, Little Star," so we learn
To be at home with forces vastly far away,
"*Ah vous dirai-je, Maman*"—how briefly

We're young—and Mozart's variations
Came true, and "Baa Baa Black Sheep," all one song.
My son can form from it his own song too
As when he sings himself to sleep each night.

The city's fogged into a frozen nebula,
Each streetlight a remote sun muffled by mist.
Alpha Centauri, our nearest star,
Is so far that to think about it hurts,

Yet we're here, singing in the very heart
Of a heavy star, together with music
To warm us, the stars we're born with
Burning until they've used themselves up.

3.

AIR AND WATER

The aquarium's a bit emptier each day.
Along the glass, a crust grows cloudier
Toward the always-nearing bottom.
Plastic Transylvanian towers and archway
Rise like volcanic islands above murkier
Depths, where a cochlear snail nestles in scum.
A Golden Comet and Fantail, two
Small fish, swim in ever-lessening space.
Memoryless, they move without history,
Gulp at floating feces, wriggle through
Ribs of a sunken galleon, poke at bloated shapes
Of ones that float, half-breathing, or already
Dead. They think it's always been this way,
Crammed in their foggy phlegm. The tank's
Floor is packed with pebbles, rainbow-stained
Like puffs of cereal, snowed over by decay,
Sloughed scales, lost fins. The golden flanks
Of those alive still glint in the nearly drained
Tank. They thrash each other for space. Today,
Water's lower. It's always been this way.

SHE ABIDES WITH ME STILL

Her tongue bristles, starred with microbes;
Eyelashes swarm with invisible locusts,

Her throat glazed with aquatic colonies,
Lush Tiergartens slung from her earlobes.

Her skin, once soft, dries and powders to dust,
Stirs to tornado with the smallest breeze

Around the Gibraltar of a bread crumb
Or Carthaginian elephant of a pincered mite.

Her eyeball is an oceanic globe.
It observes black mold behind the bottom

Bookshelves in the basement. Moths halo the light
After gnawing wool all winter in the wardrobe.

Viaducts of spider silk and confections of cat hair
Become knots of highway, archways of solar flare.

She too is a teeming empire that clings
Luckily to the surface of a rare orb,

Circling a sun that circles other suns
Like spiraled pinworms or Saturn's royal rings,

Solar systems a sponge could absorb,
Racecourses on which a gas giant runs,

Galaxies spun around by other galaxies,
Endless circlings as anonymous

As all will be in time. We're disappearing
In an endless dawn under Europa's frozen seas,

Poltergeists of angel and octopus,
Ectoplasms ninety-three earths long and then gone.

RIDDLE ME

There's only one of me
(It's not the one you see).

There's only one of me,
Even if I'm split in three.

There's only one of me
(I'm branching like a tree).

There's only one of me,
And you must have the key.

There's only one of me,
Just I and never we.

There's only one of me
(Even if you don't agree).

There's only one of me
(It's not the one you see).

MARTINI SHOT

She hasn't slept for days, and it shows.
She's two payments behind on the pink 'Vette
Parked out front in the heat. The hot
Tungsten is fierce over each tuck
And fold, her butterfly tattoo faded to flaky blue.

Air conditioning laves her skin with cold.
Her freeze-dried hair is chicken-fat yellow,
Her roots a rotten brown of peeling bark.
Her fake tan has cured to gold.

The starved-looking kid with spiked hair drives hard,
Hoping to finish on her face soon. With luck
She hopes to maybe nap, or eat. Bills are overdue,
And the season burns. She will need an ice pack.

The crew ignores her until it's over.
Big Swifty stirs seltzer into fortified wine
To brew up an ersatz champagne—
To celebrate the last shot. . . . He's done.

One tosses her a towel. The world shrinks.
She sees the water-stained ceiling and thinks
She'd like to own a ranch on a snow-lathered hill
Or a villa where gulls scream and waves spill
Around black slivers of rock. The thought scatters
Like the end of a day that feels like all the others.

THE DEMON
Stercus Diaboli

My banged-up basket
Holds a bottle of Pepto
And a lopsided avocado
Mashed black on one side,
Both on Manager's Special.

Outside, burnt-midnight Vegas
Drops Tuesday for Wednesday,
Its chasms of crazed neon
Cascading sapphires and rubies
Over bourns of black diamonds.

The self-checkout line
Smells of scorched plastic,
Shiny spills of baby oil,
Old Camels in cotton,
Puffs of Kardashian

Eau de Parfum,
And here I am again—
Tongues swollen
Out of trashed-out Nikes,
Old tube socks slack,

My cinched-up
Terrycloth bathrobe
Once an opulent blue
But now more like
A sky in the desert

Right at dawn—you might
Know what that's like—
And full KISS make-up,
Grease-paint glistening
Like fresh Cool Whip

In cool fluorescence,
Star Child tonight,
Tomorrow the Space Man,
Or the Cat, or the Demon,
My favorite, and on and on,

But it is left to tomorrow
To know for those of us
Who drive and dare
Whole lives to make
Just one beautiful thing happen.

WEST RIVER NOTEBOOK

It's just like this. Each time could be the last,
Like late November's low-angled light and the long shadows
   it knows.
That on which you work will end. The past
Is where it lives from that point on. Wind blows
Across the cold and bright of Chesapeake Bay.
The Cutty Sark's nearly gone, the wine mostly full.
The winds across the water rattle fogged casement windows,
Long ago wiped to watch oystermen pull
White skipjacks to docks and step from loaded bows.
Auden knew you are only what you want
When you work on what you love, and after that day
You might be something else or nothing. What's in front
Of you is not what you are or were. We're between
Breaths—the next not entirely ordained. That's when
And only how it lives: a moment, and what has been
May never have cause to come again,
Just as night arrives, making the water black, and we
See a sleeping ship, its lights holding it so we can see.

INTERLUDE—WEATHERING

The wind's so hard the timber groans.
Bright newborn blossoms blow like snow.
Big clouds move shadows fast on stones.
The wind's so hard the timber groans.
The storm's the thing we've always known.
What follows is what's hard to know.
The wind's so hard the timber groans.
Bright newborn blossoms blow like snow.

4.

ON CAPE CHARLES

Slab-like tankers ride at anchor.
The weakened sun still splashes acetylene
Across the water, nearly blinding me.
I swim out and surface amid the inferno,
Turn into the current and make
For the red-lensed harbor beacon
Perched high on its oil-derrick obelisk.

Foam coughs up from the jetty's black granite.
A sea-stink hangs on its edges. Floating up,
I seize the steel ladder and lug my weight
From the soapy backwash of warm water—
The lowest rungs slimy with algae
And bay grass, then the grip of dry iron
As I ascend the little lighthouse.

A great blue heron wheels and tacks.
As I reach the platform of metal mesh
The hazard strobe blazes around me
A while, goes off, and then returns.
To the south: a breakwater of half-sunken
Concrete ships, forecastles like fortress orillons,
Hulls squat on their sandbars in low waters.

The messy sunset is alive with wind.
The great marine lamp behind me
Throws its red, reflecting off
Crests as waves arrive,

Dyeing them as they ride in
Past the headland. Now my light's
The only one remaining on the bay.

In the humid dark I feel a storm move closer,
But it's impossible to know where.
It's like a weight in darkness.
I must swim back, but I stay, drying,
My beacon aimed at the night,
A signal, a warning and little else,
Until another light will show itself.

VISITATIONS

Come on in. Try our new Chicken Selects.
Forget food. We should send them luggage.
Watch this sexy star win in just five words.
Do you like who your party elects?
You could always reverse your mortgage.
A better demographic is diehard nerds.
We've never seen a storm like this before.
Get cash: Sell us your diabetes strips.
What's worse than all is that the world won't end.
Buy "Flip This House" and be a millionaire.
Call now to book amazing summer trips.
You've typed up your breakup. Now hit send.
Won't you take a moment to show you care?
We've never seen a storm like this before.
Here's one weird old trick to get rid of belly fat.
Go on. Guess who just got a Guggenheim.
It's true. Everyone says you drink too much.
A great run of growth has finally gone flat.
It's pointless in our time to use rhyme.
You really are just entirely out of touch.
We've never seen a storm like this before.
A mob has formed outside the convention.
We have no way of knowing what's kept offshore.
Please hang up now or choose an extension.
We've never seen a storm like this before.

SPOLIA OPIMA

Models, slender and famished as cheetahs,
Shed their imperial haute couture—
Already in sweatpants, they hail their cabs

Behind the Grand Palais before
Applause dies down inside around
The vacant runway. Afternoon sunlight's

Lambent overhead on friezes of Lutetian limestone.
Violinists grimace at their scores—
Haydn, Hollywood, the B's, and Broadway hits,

Rehearsal houselights hard above,
Rosin fine as cocaine settling on the boards.
They're not arrogant. They're bored.

They're paid to make the beauty go.
Why else? We all make beauty pay.
Gourmands' cheeks are all aglow as it arrives—

Voilà, another flambé. Cherries, drenched
In century-old brandy, burn like coals.
The waiter itches to check his phone. He grins.

I'm given to hyperbole, I know,
But something's got to me. It's all around.
You have to learn to make it pay you back.

The bathroom's OUT OF ORDER. Sewage seeps
Into the restaurant. The manager's
Frantic, alone today. The line's

Become a mob. A voice from an SUV
Barks at the drive-through speaker. In the back,
Children cheer a whirl of color on a screen.

I feel the boredom underneath the beauty.
It's weird, and getting desperate these days.
In auction rooms, the arms go up. And . . . sold.

The next exquisite investment's on the block.
The views—the hills, the seas—are still pristine for those
Who can afford the heights. Who's this beauty for?

Beauty's boring. I do go on and on,
Don't I? Oh, you have a nosebleed.
Here, drip some in my drink. See this?

Flick this switch. Now listen. Someone will scream.

FROM THE BALCONY
ON HEAVY METAL TRIBUTE NIGHT
AT THE TROCADERO

1870–2019

Darkness throbs below. Four teenaged women
Execute thrash metal tributes, routines of
Accomplished ferocity, furious blonde plumes
Of hair lobbed side to side on the blinding stage,
Splay-leggèd in tight jeans, knot-muscled arms
Attacking black guitars until they shriek.

I dream of vanished empires of the sea,
Lamps turned down along distant avenues,
And know I'm always partly somewhere else,
Watching Degas's ballet dancers: aslant
Like snow-loaded firs at their haunted rehearsal,
The rostrum a grotto flanked by valleys
Where nymphs sleep and hunters climb in cold shadow.

Feet in position, the singer calls the next song—
Ready to pivot at heel as she charges
Into "Ride the Lightning." Three awkward,
Aging men, thick-torsoed and gray-goateed,
Lighters aloft, nod their blunt heads at the foot
Of the stage for their fighters and fauns,
Valkyries summoning them, like memories
Of themselves, into receding vistas of smoke.

RANGE

Austrian black and weightless as a toy,
The Glock 9 almost floats in my palm

Like a water pistol purchased for a boy.
The chance of violence brings a strange calm.

Firecracker-whiffs of cordite fill the hall.
I set sights, gaze into the ruthless heat.

Gold shells flick up, clink onto concrete
And glint like ingots pinging against the wall.

The gun kicks back like an animal caught, then still,
To gather strength. The anvil'd-lead vessels

Burst the weeping eye of a paper moon, spill
No blood but give the cold feel of a kill.

This must be something more than merely a game,
Men mimicking murder, unimagined claim

To hunts and wars we feel must be
Our legacy. A shotgun thumps a galaxy

Into a human shape, echoing off the wall,
Surging on the singing seafloor of my skull.

DRINK ME

I'm so bored I'm drinking gin
From a plastic cup and blasting
Jefferson Starship. Yes. I know.
It's come to this at last.

Ice and lots of fresh towels,
The secrets of the good life,
Yet the languor of a thousand years
Lies upon me like a landslide.

Cascades of molten marble plume
Over the hectic blues of the sea,
Neptunian depths fizzling and sliding
On sands of iridescent diamond.

5.

UNION LAKE

The iron from the soil and acids from
Cedars have colored the water and leave

A fatty ochre sheen on you that dries
Into a thousand henna cataracts

Pouring into canals all down your spine.
After so much water, the wind is cold.

The afternoon is nearly gone, but darker than
It ought to be at this hour. Those who basked

Along the pine-scrub sand have gone. The boats
Have all been taken in. You leave the lake

And drive through forests to an empty house.
Once home, a shower steams, and earth and lake

Come off, a million silica, with all
The life that thrives in lakes, too small to see.

Once dried, you stretch on sheets and stare at the ceiling.
You're never washed of all that you've been in.

You haven't left the lake behind. You float
Alone there still, long after any sane

Swimmer would have left. Surviving light
Seeps away until the sky is drained,

The gloomy water growing wide, dim shores
And looming trees dissolving in the dusk.

The smell of summer lingers all around.
You feel a swipe of eel along the leg, a bump

Of cedar bough that floats, soaked thick, below
The quiet surface, more, below you, murk

Astir, a universe that loves the dark
And bears you up as if you had no weight.

REMAINS

The stag will leap in moonlight at neap tide;
Specters snake the garden paths those nights,
And wraiths are glimpsed loitering on ground
Where gallows stood in the pasture above the sea.

The castle, easily defended from all sides,
Resides high in crags, walled from the world.
All within is ruin. The keep crumbles.
The chapel, a later appendage, is half-gone

Down the mountain's face. The cistern's dried.
No chronicle survives, but the place is rumored
To have been named for a purple flower
Or two (none agreed which one it should be).

Many heirs were slain, generations lost,
Whole villages wasted and crops put to torch,
Infants impaled on spits; even a queen
Burned alive before her great mirror,

Screeching flames lighting every cold stone
Of the chamber, waving in corners
Like sunlight on the bottom of a lagoon.
The blackened circle can still be seen

On flagstones. Visitors aim their phones
Until they find it and snap the image.
Yet these are not the ghosts they claim to see.
Those who haunt these halls and frozen hills

Are not scions of the anemic family
That gradually stabbed itself out of existence.
They are really only half-happy souls
Of those who visited once, tourists, who,

On deathbeds back home, gave last thoughts
To a summer day they came to the heights,
Vacation hours that seemed to last so long,
A vivid moment of allotted time

To travel out of the tiny circuits
In which they survived as well as they could.
By day, wearing the fashions of their time,
Ghosts feed on saxifrage like bees, and evenings

Roam the rooms, or nestle before cold hearths.
It's not that they prefer the wet dark.
That's just how they're most easily seen.
They're happiest when they ride the rays

On sunny days that dry them till they're unseen,
Owning endless thoughts of escape to a place
That was only a prison or a graveyard
To others so unlike them, so long ago.

SCREAM QUEEN

I wake. The voice from the neighboring chair
Says (I must have asked), "I've always wanted
To be the Final Girl. I've had hammer claws
To the face—twice!—once dragged by my hair
Into a lake, ripped up by a haunted
Hay baler, barbequed alive by inbred outlaws,

"And, last one, acid fog caused my skin
To bubble up and made my eyelids melt."
Okay. We've all had it hard. I suppose it's work.
Clouds creep in to dull the yard, and I begin
To miss the weirdly shaped shadows that felt
So strong around the trees that droop and lurk

On the flawless lawn. The elephant ears
Are so heavy their leaves almost touch the ground.
The warm breeze can hardly even move them.
The rye grass, sage, and pines, swollen with years
Of nutrients and fertilizers, breathe all around.
I imagine the pool's chlorine colored black with chum—

It bleeds weirdly into the blue,
So deep with sadness I could dive down
My whole life and not reach the bottom. I hear
Her terriers lap at something greasy and chew.
The air goes dead. I pinch a lime and drown
Smaller cubes in gin. There's nothing to fear.

The afternoon's all used up and bruised.
The sun returns, and with it a breeze,
Sparkling the pool's surface almost white,
So stunning I have to blink to get used
To it. The shadows around the trees
Grow strong again, veiled from the light.

WE REGRET

please don't take this
the wrong way
we're wondering

is it true now we know
what you're going
to say excuse me we're

going to have to ask
that you listen I hate
to have to say this

but we've decided
and it's pretty clear-cut
you should know this is

nothing new we respect
you we do I'm
look but you knew you

were told about this we
need to talk about
we always felt something

was we know it's just
that you're I know I hate
to have to say this

APPEAL

They lead me to the dock. The courtroom's packed.
They really love me. Who draws crowds like this?
I love it when they look. And you're here too.
They think you know me after all these years,
But you don't know a thing. I'm the black hole
At the center of our galaxy. Stars eddy
And disappear as if into a drain.
I'm your very own event horizon.
Nothing you understood will make sense
Again. All rise. It's so familiar now.
The judge looks bored. They always do. I know.
And you look tired. I've got you. You can't stop
Thinking of me. And when the time arrives
To make my plea, you know what it will be.

MONSTER-MANIA CON 44

They're here where they feel safe for once,
The plush lobby of the Crowne Plaza Hotel.

Zombies are common—girls and gray-haired men,
Molars exposed wetly through sliced cheeks,

Daughters and mothers, stout and starved,
Brains bulged out of bruised skulls.

In shambolic lines up the stairs to Level Two,
Crowds flick at phones while waiting

To meet the original cast of *The Thing*.
T-Rexes get stuck in the revolving door.

My legs and skull, ballooned by Percocet,
Are buoyant as storms of gas on Jupiter.

My brother inches my antique wheelchair
Through the throng, my bandaged big toe aimed out

Like a spar on a polar icebreaker.
We bump the Creature from the Black Lagoon.

I don't feel a thing, but he snarls "do that
One *muh* time, I *shwear* . . ." from his fishy face.

Some don bold red hats emblazoned
In white "MAKE HORROR RATED R AGAIN."

So much corpse paint, so many corsets
And fishnet stockings, cats-eyes contacts,

Raven hair and Victorian jewelry;
So many living-dead girls slumped like dolls,

Seams sewn along once-severed limbs,
Who love the young men who grin to kill.

Outside, in biting wind, late sunlight cuts.
Out here, they're paler, thinner, fatter,

Pimples no longer masked by makeup, some slow
With canes, limping careful monster steps,

Killer Klowns enthroned in custom wheelchairs,
And the frightened sad glint in the eye

Of skeletal teens wondering what beasts
They can safely reach for to hug goodbye.

The cars that overflowed the lots are parked
Instead for miles along an access road.

They disappear as the sun goes out behind the trees,
Until there is only a solitary rusted Toyota

Out in the gusting cold, bumper stickers
For *Walking Dead* and *Insane Clown Posse*

On the loose rear bumper, abandoned
At an angle on the snowy mud off the asphalt

Where the long-dead grass grades down
To frost that rings like wraiths a blackened lake.

6.

Il mio core è un mar di pianti . . .

—GIACOMO CARISSIMI

ENDLESS MOUNTAINS

I wake on Easter morning in a cabin far
From home. Half dead, I sip my coffee
From an orange aluminum travel mug
And hope, with each tiny scalding sip,

To somehow regain my bearings. It's cold,
And it's my birthday. I think so little now
Of futures. I drag the past behind me
Like an overladen sled that sinks in snow.

Unbidden, my son climbs and sprawls on me.
He sees my eyes are far away and wants me back.
He kisses my cheek, holds me hard, smiling,
"I love you, daddy." Gazing past him

Out the window at distant trees loaded
With so much snow they bend and groan
I whisper (or maybe I only think)
Please love me this much forever.

LODGE

We're iced-in, this April dawn. The misted window
Hides the mountain. We've joined the ghosts who strain

To live with us inside these rooms—
They sail above the long mahogany floors, know

Stories no more than air, harboring loves slain
By time, who dined and sang, postponed their dooms.

They linger before the silent stone
Fireplace, glide down the greens. We're here

Awhile, and we imagine them. Last night,
The moon's sliver was so slender it hardly shone,

Almost melted like sugar high in the sheer
Shallow-water blue of sunset, its white

Cutting clearer as it emerged sharply
Against the tidal wash of twilight. Red

Maple and speckled alder already
Bloom here. We see them, as will others, mostly

As in a dream, and soon false hellebore
Will crowd beside the stream's insistent eddy,

Lower its lordly oars, and row.
When others arrive at the gate one day,

Will they have dreams of us, the older hosts?
They may. I hope they will. When the last snow

Goes, I know none can really stay.
Morning wanes. I've loved you, and here, as ghosts,

We lie in bed to watch the light move across
The great lawn. I want to be here to see

The starflower, still dormant—equilibrium
Of centuries on either side of us—

Unborn marsh marigold and wood anemone,
Trailing arbutus, the returning trillium.

GREAT EGRET OVER LAKE LUXEMBOURG

From its perch, almost invisible
In the rot of a red cedar snag,
A great egret, slim as a javelin,
Springs aloft and swings over us, full-
Winged and white as a noon cloud. We drag
The water, slowing, so we can see it turn.

It coasts like a balsa wood glider,
Wings stiff for stretches, spanning the lake,
Receding into a cooler shade of eastern hemlock.
Our oars of northern white ash slide
Along the mahogany coaming. When we make
Our way once more toward the dock,

They shine wet gold as bronze blades
In the sun. As we dip and pull, freshly drawn
Beads collect into clear pools that slosh
In the boat's varnished belly, catching the cascades
Of clouds overhead light as the bird, now gone.
Its flight into the air was like our push

From shore to lake, partway free.
My body lives by an element
That makes me and keeps me
Here on earth, at all times present
In an errant life skimming ever smaller years,
Filled with wax and rainforests of flora,

Slick eels and nestled snails of organs, tears
And bile, seepings beneath the aura
Of mind that makes mood, sense, and motion,
Floating in our bright, resin-sealed kayak,
Balanced by exertions, filling with a notion
Of having vanished and somehow come back.

EL CONQUISTADOR

My arbor of palo verde's alive with the hum
Of neon and cricket's whir, Sonoran wind

In the fleshy agave leaves. Two chimes
Hang over the corroded gasoline drum,

Tonic and dominant, tuned copper tubes twined
To touch and faintly ring. Sunrise limes

Hold the warmth a while. An antlered lantern
Hangs in the spidery arms of the tree,

Strands of white Christmas lights kindling stars
Through dark branches. At my ankles buckhorn

Aims out morning-star thorns. Something trailed me
Back from the desert, past wire and iron bars.

It won't let off until it's done. Late sun
Whitens the blue in an enormous corona.

Wispy clouds slip into it to disappear.
Torch aloe and lemon coral pour from pots.

What is it I hope to finally outrun?
My toddler son dabbles with dusty Arizona

Clay, making roads, smoothing them clear.
He squints as light dapples to polka dots

In the cottonwood. At last we lose the sun
Behind the shard-topped cinder blocks.

The electric strands loll in wind and run
Their light along the sides of a cube that knocks

Around my cut-crystal tumbler of Blaue Maus.
A dried white petal, living for only

A day after rain, floats from the thorn
And bark of the shrub, touches down

On the blended whiskey's bronze meniscus,
Revolves slowly like a life raft, borne

A moment until it soaks in, stained brown,
And goes under. My son begins to sing.

I can't make out the words, if they're words. We're
Safe for now. We're far from the restless sea.

We love so much. The chimes join again and ring.
My son looks up. He smiles to see I'm still here.

THE INLET
Corson's Inlet

"No swimming," warns a park ranger
From her shed on hot asphalt
Near the bridge where the sand begins.
"The Point's unguarded."
She smiles when she looks up from Peter
Matthiessen's *Wildlife in America*.

A humble bee, big and downy fuzz
Of hectic gold and coal, veers
And royally attends me, forever
In my ears as it tails me away
From its queen along the thin
Sandy trail into spiny beach scrub.

I don't understand his fascination
At first, then remember alpine flowers—
Arrowhead and aster, trefoil and nightcap—
I slipped into my hatband as I kneeled
In a blooming July meadow
At the foot of a mountain a month before.

They're dried now and trivial
As potpourri, irresistible at sea level
To my wildly alive companion.
I round a last knot of black birch
And scrub pine into slanting dune grass
To find a half-gone moon holding pale in midday blue.

The Point turns on Corson's Inlet,
Where a poet once strolled and laid down
Lines asymmetrical as a seashore.
To my south, bright jet skis blast

And bounce on broad waves
Knocking riders free.

Beer bellies, tanned all season,
Slap back onto the fiberglass rockets.
Plumes of foam go up, and they're gone
Into armadas of silver pontoons,
White diamonds of bass and bay boats,
Slow spear-tips of sail.

A massive channel dredger
Moors past sun-speckled sandbars.
I plunge and struggle out, the only one
In the surf for a mile at least,
Gaze back at the empty dunes,
Wishing I could swim out forever.

Though it feels as though I fight
The same waves in the same place,
It's not true. I, too, move.
When I look back, the beach
Is unruly with swift sandpipers
Threading a thousand tracks in sand.

I slog my way out at ebb tide,
Nightmare caught-in-clay steps
And lunges, as if withdrawing
From quicksand, forward, back
Again, and free. Salt sand stings my skin
In raw sun and frying wind.

There is no freedom in fluidity,
Only pull and toil, infinite effort
Buoyed by boundless arrangements
Of birth and loss, lure and plea,
And no real meaning but in survival
And bottomless symbols that mark it.

IN PARADISUM

The basement furnace dies at three a.m.
The chilly weather of early spring
Arrives by degrees inside the house,
Like seawater leaking into a hull.

We bundle up, treasuring our warmth.
By afternoon, the halls have chilled, as wind
Whines tunelessly and rattles at the glass.
In paradisum from Fauré's Requiem

Chimes down the crooked stairs like lazy stars
Revolving overhead, pining away
For me, yearning to have me home again,
Out there shining in solar Sargassos,

Or ocean swirls of discarded plastic
Gathering in Pacific emptiness.
Fresh dust snows on the furniture and floor. I breathe
The busy air, teeming with life, split by shafts

Of sunlight. My voice is dry from all the dust.
It's taken over everything. It coats
The meniscus of my glass of water.
It's made of us, our cats and candles—

Rumors of how our lives will be consumed—
Particles of meteor and pollen,
The powder that appears on the floorboards
When nails are hammered into old walls—

Iridescent archipelagos of pearl
Trailing lagoons of chalk white in their wakes.
Our self-incineration, which hardly hurts,
Starts lightning racing into nothingness.

I know we're dust, and stardust too, but more—
Phosphorescent in oceans of sunlight,
Like breaths exhaled, diffusions, traces of song,
Engines firing in the voiceless dark.

7.

ἔνθα δύω νύκτας δύο τ' ἤματα κύματι πηγῷ
πλάζετο, πολλὰ δέ οἱ κραδίη προτιόσσετ' ὄλεθρον.
ἀλλ' ὅτε δὴ τρίτον ἦμαρ ἐυπλόκαμος τέλεσ' Ἠώς,
καὶ τότ' ἔπειτ' ἄνεμος μὲν ἐπαύσατο ἠδὲ γαλήνη
ἔπλετο νηνεμίη

—THE ODYSSEY

ALCHEMERICANA

He's shipwrecked far from realms he knew, a king
Abandoned in winter, promised rescue,
Breathing turned-earth gusts of manure
Poured from far-off fields still fallow in spring.

The winds bring back old moods he'd hoped were gone,
Cartographic mayhem of newfound shores
That seemed to move each night, slow palms at dawn,
Hot stones, the gathering sun, the lick of oars.

Once back inside he wonders if you set
Aside thoughts of him, searches the icebox,
Finds a foggy Ziploc bag with broken blocks
Of Dino Chicken behind a Hot Pocket—

Crystal-crusted in their plastic cavern.
Shaken out, a single ice-rock lump hits
The bowl. It slips apart and starts to sweat,
Soaking microwaveable light each turn.

Behold: a feast, dumped over steaming
Intestines, a bed of boiled Ramen,
The last packet in the cupboard. Well then,
Much better. A stranded lord is dreaming

Of what must vanish, slow down, diminish,
Of lives—once planned far out ahead—now blurred,
Of shapes in failing sight, a word once slurred,
Of a fall day he will not live to finish.

SALVAGING

I try to fall asleep. I turn myself
To face the fan, imagine that it's wind.
Tomorrow might be better. It must. It's not.
It's not. It never is, and still I lie

Like a body washed up from a schooner
Foundering in an old lithograph. The tide
Is rising fast to pull me out again.
I try to fall asleep. I turn away.

My feet protrude, chilled like winter marble.
Wreckers tramp eagerly all around me,
Boots sucking in loosened sand. They pull
Up flotsam from the waves, crates and bottles,

Stepping right over me, lanterns swinging
All around in the degenerate darkness—
I stare into a starless whistling of sky,
Envisioning worlds I might make my own,

Stories I'd fashion from this very air,
Released to waters rising cold as space,
The great final dream of being let go
From a body that does not want me.

MINERAL SPRINGS TRAIL

Our boy raises the fern's vivid array in a ceremonial way,
Its spine curved by its own small weight, its apex waving almost
Imperceptibly in a humid breeze, pinnules cut like crystals

Climbing from a cavern floor, a blade acute as a glaive wielded
Across a field of war. Late sunlight rumoring through hemlocks
Ignites it like a torch an instant in shifting shadows.

He sets the still wet stem of the frond in the clean hollow
Of a deer femur he salvaged searching among granite
That rose to a grotto carved by springs over a million years

Into the mountainside. He leads us down steps molded
   by roots, scepter
At his side: Prince of Ferns, you will rule here forever in this one
Moment of your tiny courage—may you learn to live by it,

And may we be allowed to abide here with you as long as we may
In our memories, and follow you down, and be as brave as you,
As we make our way, day by day, into deepening darkness.

71

DEEP SHADE

1.

Every garden should keep a grave,
    A mortal seed below
The weeds and grass, beds of tulips,
    A force that might bestow
A nutrient putrefaction
    For those on top that grow:

A household cat, wrapped up in a towel,
    An odoriferous
Shape shrinking each year, or goldfish
    Becoming glutinous
In shade of boughs that overhang
    To keep the sun from us—

A beloved family dog,
    A once magnificent horse,
A hamster in a jewelry box,
    The things that lost their force,
Any sort of heart-stilled creature
    Returning to its source.

2.

Some clouds will cross the yard. Some gusts
    Will move the apple tree,
And spread the light that turns all day
    In patches slipping free
Like thoughts that fail to find a shape.
    I really should not try

To understand the end, and neither
        Should you—and why would we?—
I fear we may have leaned enough
        On love and come to see
That strengths on which we now depend
        Will someday cease to be.

3.

The songs we work to memorize
        Will finally disperse
Until they're noise, then silence.
        No song that we rehearse
Can slow the universal decline
        That nothing can reverse.

4.

Could it be that love and death are roots,
        Together feeling for
A reservoir to drink, to find
        A saving drop or spore,
Some sustenance beneath the earth,
        A nourishment; or

Are they really branches ramified
        Further into smaller
Twigs, sending down their fruits,
        Growing ever taller,
Ever higher from the body
        Dwindling in its collar?

IN SALT MEADOWS

Blood ark and aster, gale-flattened bulrush,
Purple loosestrife, stargazer, and coffin box,
Summer airstream, arrow worm, and oystercatcher,
Father Sunset, while we stay here sing us that song—

Your sons, brittle star, surf, and firethorn bush,
Conifers and carp, catfish, speck of hawk,
Bog rot, grub, great-tailed grackle, egg snatcher,
Sudden damselfly, bull shark, sturgeon, tooth and prong—

Your daughters deadly too, sedge and sea rocket, raccoon,
Last of sun igniting runnels, lava flow
To bay swollen with sponge, mosquito, and mudfish—
Sing of sorrows, cyphers, corals, and crows,

Ghost crab, nettle, anemone, moist moon
Bloomed to mushroom cap, glasswort, silvery minnow—
Rainwater course with salt, mixed like a wish,
The stories we survive, salt grass, and swamp rose.

SOLE UNQUIET THING

Afraid to sleep tonight alone, he joins us
In our bed, scrambling over pillow peaks
And furrows of bunched-up blanket.
Overtired at this hour, he clowns for us
And laughs. He balls the sheet and smiles,
"Look, a wave!" For him, it *is* a wave, and back

He falls, sunk into white. He lolls between us
And falls asleep while scritching my new beard
With tiny hands. I drift a while but wake
To find his hand in mine. Where is he now?
He's far from me, I feel, the more we touch.
I smile to wind up here in our very own darkness

With him. My dreams are thefts, my life halfway
Used up. He pulls his hand from mine, abounding
In waves, cut off from me in his own dream.
Time bobs in me—the past mere jetsam—
My tired body a dirty tide struggling
Against some moon of my own lost joys,

So much exhaustion of earth and empires.
What journeys has he undertaken while we slept?
Soon drizzly light will seep its way through blinds,
Leaking into the clockless hour before
The alarm and coming of day that sours
Our time and all the hopes we've sorrowed over.

Sleep well. One day you'll swim these storms yourself.
There will be snow to cover the wet stones,
And mists arisen to steal the horizons.
Rest, my son. There is always sunlight and sea,
And gales that sweep the margins of our world,
And tall trees lit by lightning in the night.

CPSIA information can be obtained
at www.ICGtesting.com
Printed in the USA
LVHW040842300123
738071LV00001B/10